SEXMATTERS

LOVE, MARRIAGE, AND THE SUNNAH

MUSLIMMATTERS

O humanity! Be mindful of your Lord Who created you from a single soul, and from it He created its mate, and through both He spread countless men and women.

And be mindful of Allah—in Whose Name you appeal to one another—and honor family ties. Surely Allah is ever Watchful over you.

The Holy Qur'an 4:1

CONTENTS

The Sunnah of the Prophet 🌸 is rich with love and its many expressions, so how did sternness and lack of affection come to be associated with religiosity?

We're still growing as a couple, in love and with love. MashaAllah. And the years behind us may have rushed past, but the years ahead stretch before us with possibility and potential.

Virginity and bloody bed sheets- are these the cultural conditions that make a good Muslim marriage?

After the nikkah is it permissible to do all the acts that are permissible between a husband and wife, even if the rukhsati hasn't been done?

ON SECRET MARRIAGES

Secret marriage is one of several kinds of violations by men of the rights and dignity of women.

WHEN HE LEAVES FOR HER: AN UNACCEPTED REALITY IN OUR COMMUNITIES

I'll never forget the morning I found out that my husband was having an emotional affair with one of my close friends.

Dear Reader,

I am delighted to introduce the first edition of a compilation of essays published on MuslimMatters about what touches our hearts, our senses and our souls. In a way, that should not be unexpected —we are a forum that touches all aspects of Muslim life.

Here we will traverse through Prophetic Love to some difficult topics: same-sex attraction, sexless marriage, and secret marriage. These need to be read and discussed, and we hope this book will help facilitate some discussions and clear up misconceptions.

The Prophet ﷺ loved our mother Aisha [ranha]— "like a strong binding knot," the harder a knot is pulled, the stronger the bond gets. Prophetic love teaches us love in difficult times, and shows us the way to hold tight to each other. The Muslim community is as diverse in its challenges as it is in its successes, and trust us, MuslimMatters.org should know.

Since 2007, we've had the honor of publishing many critical conversations from, and about the Muslim community and it's not all about love. Sometimes it's about hate. Sometimes it's about anti-Muslim bigotry, government policies, and the confusing balance between political involvement and religious rights.

Other times, it's about faith and the conflict between first culture, second generation, and third spaces. MuslimMatters.org is a not-for-profit organization dedicated to the voices of scholars, artists, writers, and activists from the Muslim world. That means our work is as diverse as our faith.

We thank Allah for this opportunity and ask Him for the privilege of continuing it. We would also like to thank the writers and scholars who have given us permission to reprint their work.

And to you, dear reader, JazakAllahukhairan. Your purchase of this book is a key part of MuslimMatters.org's financial and ideological independence. Your support keeps our website free, allowing over a million Muslims every year to access content from some of the best and brightest writers in our Ummah. It also gives us the independence to publish any discussion with an Islamic basis, not just the ones with sponsor support.

To learn more about how you can support these and other important conversations, visit muslimmatters.org/support. For information on this and other publications, visit muslimmatters.org/books.

JazakAllahuKheiran,

Hena Zuberi
Editor in Chief
MuslimMatters.org

THE SUNNAH OF LOVE

By Shaykh Yahya Adel Ibrahim

I get messaged often from couples trying to salvage and mend broken trust and exponentially inhospitable relationships. I usually respond within a couple of weeks, detailing my unwillingness to "counsel" from a virtual distance that begets unilateralism. Horror stories of infidelity, violence, and arrogance abound. Naturally, there is no greater issue facing the Muslim communities of the West that is more pressing and multidimensional than that of family relations.

The statistics are frightening, imams are untrained in effective counseling methods, mosques are under pressure, Islamically-oriented marital counselors are unheard of and professionalism in terms of confidentiality seem non-existent.

An important dimension of domestic marital problems, as I see, is that the Sunnah of Love and Gallantry seems to be overlooked or dismissed as a long-gone era. We seem to overlook amazing instances of passion, valor, fidelity and sacrifice in the name of true love, even as the

Sunnah is full of instances from the life of the Prophet ﷺ and his companions that build a comprehensive system of devotion – a Sunnah of Love.

Love. The real kind

Houb - love - in Arabic is derived from the same root for the word *Haab* – seed. The nature of the two words is functionally similar. A seed, literally and figuratively, symbolizes love. Genuine love between a man and his wife stems from a seed of love, planted by Allah in the hearts of those who are true in submission to the Dispenser of Love and Comfort.

Love begins as a tiny speck - a seed that is buried deep in the folds of a receptive heart, carrying the potential of stunning beauty, nourishing sustenance, exotic delicacy, wealth of commodity, shading shelter, and resurgent growth that is stabilized through deep roots that withstand trauma.

Amr ibn al-'As, may Allah be pleased with him, was appointed by the Prophet to command an important mission. He was handpicked from many capable individuals who were in fact better than him. Feeling a sense of pride in being selected, Amr asked the Prophet, in front of a congregation of Sahabah about who he ﷺ, loved, hoping to hear his own name. The Prophet ﷺ responded in the way that all of our wives would hope we would respond, by naming his wife, Aisha.

Consider that the Prophet would teach that if we love a friend, we need to let them know it. It was with this hope that 'Amr thought to ask that question after a favorable appointment was given to him.

Thinking that his question has been misunderstood Amr clarified, saying that he meant from amongst the companions. The Prophet ﷺ responded, "Her Father."

Aisha's father was his best friend and confidant Abu Bakr, but instead of naming him, the Prophet's framing of Abu Bakr as "her father" tells us that 'Aisha was still on his mind and in his heart.

Love

'Aisha, al-Humayra – The Rosy Cheeked one, as the Prophet affectionately called her; *Umm al-Mu'mineen* – the Mother of the Faithful was loved and loved in return.

The Sunnah of Love is not whimsical or outrageously simplistic as you find depicted often in multibillion-dollar literary/theatrical sagas. No vampires competing with werewolves here. It is not ambivalent and shifty. It is built on mutual acceptance of the decree of the Divine in search of comfort, repose, and peace of mind.

It flourishes, paradoxically, in the mundanity of life, finding fleeting moments of intimacy between stacks of dishes, soiled diapers, mounds of work emails, grocery lists and infinite commitments are its hallmark. A look that you receive as you rush out the door, a quick phone call itemizing how the day is going or an SMS that contains a list of groceries to buy on the way home punctuated with an I love You, are all indicators.

'Aisha *raḍyAllāhu 'anh*a and the Prophet ﷺ would use coded language with each other denoting their love. She asked the Prophet how he would describe his love for her. The Prophet Muhammad answered, saying: "Like a strong binding knot." The more you tug, the stronger it gets.

Every so often 'Aisha would playfully ask, "How is the knot?" The Prophet would answer, "As strong as the first day (you asked)."

So I begin to wonder, what has happened to our community?

Why is it so hard to speak frankly of one's love for his wife? Why is it considered "soft" for a brother to praise his spouse?

How is it the Prophet can kiss his wife as he exits to leave his home to lead the faithful in prayer, and some in our community find it difficult to just smile?

Since when is sternness considered leadership and harshness associated with married life?

How is it that the Prophet can mend his clothes and look after the domestic affairs of his household, and a brother can't put away a plate, let alone wash it unless the wife is sick?

How is it that the Prophet can forbid upon himself milk infused with honey so as to please his wives, who complained of its scent, culminating in Allah revealing a chapter in the Qur'an forbidding the Prophet from forbidding the lawful upon himself, "Because you seek to please your wives (66:1)." Yet, some in our community will not even give the rightfully due to their wife?

How is it that the Prophet not to boycott a person for more than three days, and a brother can be out all day at work and feel apprehensive at the thought of returning home to a disgruntled partner who will give them the silent treatment over a petty squabble that has extended into weeks of dreary, isolating depression?

How is it that the Prophet *ṣallallāhu 'alayhi wa sallam* forbids a person to lead another man in prayer in his home without permission, yet some brothers due to constant bickering and negative criticism feel more like the help than the king of the castle?

How is it that the Prophet can stop a whole army - in times of hostility and a region of the desert that had no water to camp near- to look for his wife's misplaced bead necklace, and some find it difficult to give a deserved compliment every now and again?

All of us learn through the course of our elementary studies of Islam that if you have no water, or if it is scarce, that you can perform *Tayamum* – ritual purification for prayer using sand or dust. What you probably were not taught, and what was glossed over, was the fact that the permissibility and the legislation of that enormously important function were revealed because of the lost bead necklace.

You were not told that the love of the Prophet *ṣallallāhu 'alayhi wa sallam* for 'Aisha resulted in him ordering a marching army to stop at a location without water and camp out at night with a dwindling supply of water for their consumption. Her father, Abu Bakr *raḍyAllāhu 'anhu*, was furious with her for mentioning what, to him, seemed to be a trivial matter.

You were not told how the Prophet *ṣallallāhu 'alayhi wa sallam* ordered the troops to look for a necklace in the sands of the Arabian Desert, all for the comfort of 'Aisha. You were, probably, not informed how verses in the Qur'an descended upon the Prophet at such an occasion resulting in the joyous celebration of the Sahabah for the ease that Allah has provided for our *Ummah* as a result of this occurrence. Misreading the Sunnah, and not linking it to all matters of our life, including the mundane aspects is a justified criticism of those who are not teaching it to its full depth.

That is the Sunnah of Love. You look after the near, even if it may inconvenience the far.

You would have heard that the Prophet *ṣallallāhu 'alayhi wa sallam* mended his own shoes at times. What you may not have heard was how once as he was sitting in a room with 'Aisha *raḍyAllāhu 'anha* fixing his shoes, 'Aisha happened to look to his blessed forehead and noticed that there were beads of sweat on it. Mesmerized by the majesty of that sight she remained transfixed staring at him long enough for him to notice.

The Prophet *ṣallallāhu 'alayhi wa sallam* said, "What's the matter?" She replied, "If Abu Bukair Al-Huthali, the poet, saw you, he would know that his poem was written for you." The Prophet *ṣallallāhu 'alayhi wa sallam* asked, "What did he say?" She replied,

"Abu Bukair said that if you looked to the majesty of the moon, it twinkles and lights up the world for everybody to see."

So the Prophet *ṣallallāhu 'alayhi wa sallam* got up, walked to Aisha, kissed her between the eyes, and said,

"*Wallahi* ya Aisha, you are like that to me and more."

That is the Sunnah of Love

From the earliest days of Islam, 'Ali radiya Allahu 'anhu was a continuous witness of the life habits of Rasool-ul-Allah *ṣallallāhu 'alayhi wa sallam*. He was a witness to Love.

Ali came home one day from a journey that he had been dispatched on by the Prophet Muhammed *ṣallallāhu 'alayhi wa sallam*, to find his wife, Fatima, the daughter of the Prophet, *radiya Allahu 'anha* brushing her teeth with a *siwak* – twig of an Arak (Salvadora persica) tree. He recited to her poetic endearment:

Fortunate are you O twig of the Arak tree,
Have you no fear of me observing you in this embrace
If it were other than you...O Siwak!
I would have killed you!
None found this fortune of embrace before me, but you.

To what do we owe the occasion of this poem? There was no foreshadowing of anything special about the occasion or day. There was no fancy marketing to fleece customers of hard earned money. There were no gimmicks or convoluted infatuations promising a happily ever after proportional to carat size. There was just a man – Ali - coming home after a long day at work. What he finds there is the greatest attainment any man could dream to possess, and hopefully retain – a wife whose presence fills him with joy.

The Prophet Muhammad, *ṣallallāhu ʿalayhi wa sallam*, said: "The world and all things in the world are precious but the most precious thing in the world is a virtuous woman."

Virtuous, not, exclusively, in terms of the length of prostration or in devotion to religious obligations but rather as he, *ṣallallāhu ʿalayhi wa sallam*, once informed ʿUmar:

"Shall I not inform you about the best treasure a man can hoard? It is a virtuous wife who fills him with joy whenever he looks towards her."

It is not love at first sight, rather exponential love with every glance.

Ya Allah, put love between our spouse and us and allow us comfort and mercy in our home.

Ya Allah, spread love and peace throughout the *Ummah* of Muhammed *ṣallallāhu ʿalayhi wa sallam*

O Allah grant us Your Divine Love

O Allah grant us the love of those who Love You

O Allah grant us the love of doing the things that earn Your Divine Love

Shaykh Yahya Ibrahim is serving member of the Board of Directors for MuslimMatters.org. He is a specialist in spirituality and the Qur'an, having studied Tafsir, Fiqh and Hadith with scholars from Hijaz and Egypt.

He frequently educates on domestic violence, misogyny, gender discrimination, child protection, disability and mental health. A recipient of the West Australian Multicultural Community Service Award for Individual Excellence, Shaykh Yahya serves the Muslim community at Curtin University and the University of Western Australia as the Islamic Chaplain and teaches Islamic Ethics & Theology, internationally, with al-Kauthar Institute www.alkauthar.org

TEN YEARS, TEN REFLECTIONS ON MARRIAGE

By Hiba Masood

A couple of years before I got married, I was at a bridal shower where there was a short talk on marriage by the bride's very learned old aunt. One of the women present remarked that she had been married for ten years and felt very experienced herself and the aunt replied with a gentle laugh, "Ten years? Ten years is nothing. You need about forty years of marriage to really understand yourself and the other person."

At the time, I recall sniffing a little disdainfully. What was this lady going on about? Ten years was an absolute *lifetime* with a person. I imagined myself being married for ten years and I could see the wisdom and experience practically *dripping* off of me. Well, now, I've been married for ten years and the only true knowledge that I have is: Ten years is nothing. But here is a little something anyway.

1. Rinse, rest, repeat

Many a things are made better or cured completely by a few tears, a little sugar, a long shower, a good night's sleep or, ideally, all four. You know how everyone says don't go to sleep angry? I say boo to that. A smarter strategy: Cry in the shower, eat some chocolate, head to bed. Do not stay up to fight. Anger + sleepy fatigue = Bad news. It much wiser to call timeout, establish a temporary peace on whatever the issue of the hour is so that there are no angels cursing you all night and go to sleep. In the morning, the sun will stream through the windows and through the dark recesses of your mind, and everything will seem brighter. You might just pick up where you left off but there is also a *really* good chance that you can't be bothered any more and would much rather concentrate on the scrambled eggs with chives that you've just cooked up.

2. Expect the unexpected

Marriage is a lot like parenting in that it's always something new. In parenting, just when you have mastered the infant stage, your child becomes a toddler. Just when you figure out the basics of bedtime routines and potty training, your kid turns around and tells you he wants to major in Theories and Subcultures of Aztec Dance.

Marriage is exactly the same. Odd and unpredictable. Every couple is forever a work in progress. The spouses will grow and evolve as individuals and the only job of the marriage is to make sure that growth is, on the balance, more towards each other than apart.

In my own marriage, Hums has been a surprise to me at every single turn of our life together. There have been many disappointments. But I keep the faith because the surprises haven't been all bad. After years of buttering his toast and making sure his shirt collar was ironed just so, I had boxed him into the tidy category of "good hearted, slightly feudal, blissfully unaware of feminism and the ensuing equality of the sexes and division of household chores that entails."

Then suddenly, to my utter disbelief and unbridled joy, one fine morning in our seventh year, Hums turned around and began making me dinner every Friday and Saturday night. That he, with his roasted fennel stuffed sea bass, and perfectly fluffy crème brulees, turned out to be a far superior cook than I had ever been, was the icing on a very sweet cake and has definitely brought us closer. I mean, *how could it not?!*

3. You are far too complicated for one person

The ideal soul mate spouse is one who shares every interest, gets every joke, hangs on to every word that drops from our rosebud lips, wants to spend every waking minute with us and fervently desires for us every last exact thing that we desire for ourselves no matter to what personal cost.

Unfortunately, the actual spouse is too busy flossing his teeth while watching a televised sport you loathe and Whatsapping a friend you consider totally lame to pay much attention to your totally hilarious chicken joke.

Marrying Hums gave me a partner, a provider, a dinner buddy, a shopping bag carrier, a weekend movie companion and my most favorite secret keeper. We've really nailed the being each other's garment. But there's lots and lots it didn't give me, because there's no such thing as one soul mate.

My soul (and anyone's soul) is too multi faceted for any one person to satisfy. Fulfilling every part of my personality is too great a burden for one person to bear. Hums fills the husband shoes pretty okay. But thankfully, I've got my siblings and cousins and friends and professional colleagues for everything else. God is Great.

4. Love is a language

And just because you're living together doesn't mean you speak the same language. I spent the early days of my marriage wondering if I would ever get the grand gestures and surprise gifts that felt to me to be the epitome of romance.

Now, I relish Hums's small expressions of tenderness and I derive great satisfaction from knowing that only I am privy to his careful and particular demonstrations of thoughtfulness. He has his own way of speaking love and through time, I have learned to listen, and to distinguish his vernacular from the noisy chatter of my own expectations.

Marriage demands you be willing to accept love in the way it is offered and give it in the way that it desired, and meet halfway between expectations and abilities. Sometimes you will be lucky and the way you want love is the way your spouse gives it. But more often, over the years you slowly craft your own gibberish and with practice, it becomes the sweetest song you ever did hear.

5. Look at the bigger picture

The trick to surviving and thriving in your marriage is to always take the long view, not the immediate one.

There have been days in which I have spent a good hour or so of my life imagining, in great detail, life without Hums. Sometimes, because, if he hasn't answered three of my phone calls, I am convinced he is lying dead on the side of the highway somewhere. But other times, because after a particularly tense conversation, I decide I want to leave him.

I tell myself, Allah is my witness, life with this man is completely unbearable, he has never *once* understood me, I am far better off alone, living and working on my art, in some secluded little town in the south of Spain where nobody knows my name and they refer to me as that "mysterious woman writer with the sad eyes and brave smile."

A couple of hours after chalking out an elaborate exit plan, complete with dramatic grabbing of the passport and sweeping out the door without a backward glance, Hums comes home, pats my hand like an absent minded professor, winking as he compliments the chicken curry, and with a whoosh, I am back, physically, emotionally and spiritually, thanking Allah that the overly zoomed-in moment has passed and no life altering decisions had been taken in it.

When I keep my eye on the bigger picture under formation, I know Hums and I have joked and laughed and jumped around in the pouring rain. We've been to Umrah and every Muslim wife knows that their man in an Ihram, standing, at night, under the glittering lights of the Haram courtyard is a heartwarming sight that can fill you up with gratitude for days. We've held hands lightly, barely grazing palms, while strolling through parks and we've held hands tightly, almost crushing each other's bones, when the doctor diagnosed our son with multiple delays, when our daughter went in for eye surgery, when the news came that my father was seriously unwell.

In all reasonably functional marriages, the good times far, far outweigh the bad times but that clarity only comes with stepping back from the canvas of your life and gazing, awestruck, at the masterpiece that is slowly taking shape.

6. Dua helps and heals

Even if your duas are not answered, in a way or shape that you prefer, there is something creatively self fulfilling about the very act.

When you let yourself be weak and you empty out your heart in dua, your heart feels full and strong again. When your heart feels full and satisfied after dua, you remember that only the remembrance of Allah, not your spouse, can give your heart satisfaction. Thus you remember Him more. Praying for my marriage has made me more appreciative of it. Praying for Hums has made me more grateful for his presence in my life. Feeling grateful and appreciative has made me pray more and happily so.

It's a lovely little circular thing which grows bigger in scope over time and great for any marriage. A little dua every day keeps the doctor, the doldrums and the desperate desire to escape away.

7. All conversations are not created equal

Contrary to what most people advise about talking it all out, I don't think that every conversation needs to be brought to it's reasonable and complete conclusion. Some things are better left unsaid.

Ten years of being missus to the very quiet Hums has shown me the power of the unuttered. Many, many things self resolve. Situations that seem concrete often turn out theoretical. Talking about the what-ifs, the future, anything but the precise present moment can sometimes be a great bonding exercise and other times a ticking bomb best left untouched. Learning to recognize the difference took me the better part of ten years but I'm glad I'm finally there.

8. Sex: Don't take it too seriously

It is a strange beast and it is adept as a shape shifter. The sexual intimacy in your marriage can be awesome and it can be bad. It can bring you together and it can tear you apart. It can be a constant, steady feature of your marriage, say, twice a week, every week and then bam, you have a baby and a killer episiotomy and it vanishes for months, disappearing without a trace, acting for all practical purposes as if it has never existed.

The only way to always come back into your sexual groove as a couple, is to not take any of it too seriously. Don't let its shape shifting abilities pull a fast one over you. Laugh off the mishaps and misunderstandings, forgive the miscommunications and misdemeanors and try again. Sex is a highly essential and integral part of a healthy, happy marriage, extremely important to the sanity and stability of the individuals and the couple, powerful in it's ability to aid reconciliation and heal growth, but at the end of the day, it's just sex. Shrug it off and try again.

9. One or two common interests is plenty

It takes two to tango, they say, but what they don't say is that sometimes you can each dance to a different beat and still be in perfect harmony.

Hums and I are as different as night and day. On most things, our views are worlds apart and this may have a lot to do with the fact that we were born and raised worlds apart. But we both love good food and American politics and we'd both rather spend money on books than anything else and these few shared interests have given us ten years of great meals, terrific conversations and a book collection to be proud of, even at a time when we didn't have enough money to pay the grocery bills. On common interests we are seamless, on separate interests we've each found our own outlets.

Home is where our stories begin but they don't need to always end there. A far richer narrative is created when each of the spouses bring their own voice to the table.

10. Forgive

Which is precisely the beautiful, God-given gift of marriage: Forgiveness. Every day, you wake up in the morning and you turn and see the same face beside you, offering in its constant and loyal presence, redemption from all the flukes, foibles and follies of the day before.

Every day is another opportunity to start over, to get it right, to reaffirm that who you were as a couple the previous day doesn't have any implication on who you can be today. Your happy marriage can begin the very morning, the very moment you choose it to. Allah is Al-Kareem and how awesomely generous of Him to give us these second chances, all these fresh opportunities to create better, wiser, lists and litanies of what makes for a happy marriage. What a gift.

Even though we've been together ten years, I am just getting to know this man. I know how he was as a young man in his twenties trying to figure out his new bride. I know how he was in his early thirties as a father to three young kids. I know how he was recently during a period of long unemployment. I don't know if he will have a midlife crisis in a few years time. I don't know how he will be when its time for the kids to go to college. I don't know how he will be when one of us loses a parent or is struck with a life changing illness. He is, like me, like us, a work in progress. There's so much about him I don't know. Every day is a brand new introduction.

The last decade has been a blur of work and babies and diapers and figuring out how to work in order to afford all those diapers for all those babies. The years with Hums have rushed by and some days, when my heart is feeling particularly tender and his hair is looking particularly salty and not so peppery, I experience a sudden choking.

Did we miss it all because we were just too busy? Did I allow myself to sideline the chemistry between us? Did I let the crying children drown out his voice, the voice of this man that I am, at this very moment, feeling so madly in love with? Verily by the passage of time we have been at a loss! How can I do better by him? *Oh, I must do better by him, I must!* A couple more of these grandly regretful thoughts and I find myself getting misty eyed and nostalgic. Only when Hums grumbles something about his undershirts *always* missing from the drawer and can I *ever* remember the laundry, do I roll my eyes and tell myself to calm down.

Because, even as I secretly vow to do better, I remind myself of the Will of Allah and how it can manifest in ways that can be so surprising. There's so much ahead that I don't know yet about our life together and Hums as a person.

You know, I wasn't very nice to Hums yesterday. We didn't end the day on the best of notes. But today? Today our song, our story, our work of art, is going to be so beautiful. Because, we're still alive and together. Alhumdulillah. We're still growing as a couple, in love and with love. MashaAllah. And the years behind us may have rushed past, but the years ahead stretch before us with possibility and potential. InshaAllah.

Author's note: Writing on marriage always carries a certain burden of responsibility towards the audience. The writer is never sure who out there is reading under what circumstances the apparently sage and often flippant "advice".

This here then is my disclaimer: All of what I say applies only to your every day, run of the mill reasonably happy marriages between two good people. Any and all of the below is complete garbage if there is infidelity, criminal activity, haraam tendencies or genuine physical, emotional or sexual abuse taking place in a marriage.

No amount of positivity, good intentions or light heartedness can remedy unions damaged by these things, except by the Will of Allah. May He protect us all from the fitnah of difficult marriages and bless our good unions with His Mercy.

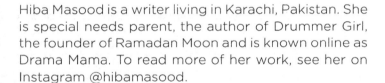

Hiba Masood is a writer living in Karachi, Pakistan. She is special needs parent, the author of Drummer Girl, the founder of Ramadan Moon and is known online as Drama Mama. To read more of her work, see her on Instagram @hibamasood.

ON BLOODY BACKWARD BED SHEETS

By Zainab Bint Younus

Virginity and bloody bed sheets- are these the cultural conditions of what make a good Muslim marriage? A quick Google search will yield hundreds of results – the majority focusing on the European phenomenon of women from Muslim families seeking "certificates of virginity" and/or hymen restoration surgery before they get married.

Debates rage on about European Muslims importing such cultural backwardness as vaginal blood on newlyweds' bed sheets to be proof of the bride's virginity, affecting the generation of youth born and brought up on Western soil. Reading these stories, several things come to mind. The situation isn't just about women's virginity; it's about many societal ills that the Muslim community is facing.

Ignorance is a contributing factor to this sensitive issue, on many levels. Far too many people believe that a woman's hymen is destroyed by intercourse alone. The truth is, however, that accidents, physical activity, and even everyday movements can result in the 'puncturing' of hymens. Thus, the expectation of vaginal blood as proof of virginity is a faulty one that cannot be relied upon for accuracy.

The entire concept of "proof of virginity" is alien to the Deen and completely absent in the Shari'ah. The only Islamically acceptable way of knowing whether someone has committed Zina (fornication) is by confession, or having been caught fornicating by the required four witnesses, making the whole idea of physiological "proof" redundant.

Furthermore it is commanded of both Muslim men and women to abstain from pre-marital relations. The double standards that demand proof of the bride's virginity –and not a groom's, are another sign of culture being placed over religion. Many families are willing to turn a blind eye to their sons "playing the field", but become borderline psychotic if their daughters are caught doing so.

It seems that in many cases, the women (and men) involved in these dramas may not be very practicing to begin with, hence the virginity-proving dilemma. In at least one case, a boyfriend and girlfriend were engaged to marry, but then the groom's family demanded proof of the bride's virginity. Clearly, to them, proof of (technical) virginity was more important than the fact that their son had been dating the same girl for some time already.

It must be clearly understood that the Shari'ah does not differentiate between male and female when it comes to gender relations and sexual conduct. Premarital relationships are 100% forbidden. It isn't "worse" if a woman commits zina, or "not as bad" if a man does. In both cases, it is haram and the gravity of the sin is equal in the eyes of Allah.

Sheikh Yaser Birjas kindly provides us with a scholarly overview of the issue:

> "Asking for a 'virginity test' is something new in the Muslim society. It's hard to find anything regarding this issue in such a straight forward manner in classical works of fiqh, for such a request implies suspicion in the chastity of the woman and hence falls under 'Qadhf' – meaning false accusation. This request is not only a violation to her body, but also to her innocence and to her honor.
>
> If the man or his family were suspicious of the virginity of a woman then they should dissolve the contract rather than demanding such request. This request springs from fear of shame on the part of the groom or his family. They do not wish to be accused of calling off a marriage for no reason for fear of the social backlash.
>
> The "bloody bedsheets' tradition is absolutely haram, awful and works against the request of Rasulullah ﷺ to keep intimate matters private. The Messenger of Allah said,

"Verily among the worst people before Allaah on the Day of Judgement is a man who approaches his wife sexually and she responds and then he spreads her secrets."

In another narration, Asmaa bint Yazid reported that she was once in the presence of the Prophet and there were both men and women sitting. The Prophet said: "Perhaps a man might discuss what he does with his wife, or perhaps a woman might inform someone what she did with her husband?"

The people were silent. Asma then said: "O, Yes! O Messenger of Allah verily both the women and men do that."

Then the Prophet said: "Do not do that. It is like a male shaitaan who meets a female shaitaan along the way, and has sex with her while the people look on!"

If speaking about what happens between a husband and wife behind closed doors was made haram per the statements of Rasulullah (sallallaahu 'alayhi wa sallam), what about showing it or putting it on display?

The rules of Shariah are based on 'sitr,' a concept that entails concealing moral blemish when possible and promoting chastity. Therefore, unmarried women are assumed to be virgins unless evidence suggests

> *otherwise. Women are not obligated to prove their virginity."*

The matter is clear: there is nothing in the Shari'ah that requires physiological 'proof' of female virginity via the demonstration of hymen blood. Rather, the entire concept of demanding such proof goes against Islamic values and sexual ethics, which presume the default sexual innocence of believing women (and men), unless proven otherwise through the rigorous and demanding process of providing four eyewitnesses who have seen the physical act of intercourse take place between two people.

The practice of using hymen blood as 'proof' of female virginity result is incredibly damaging on both an individual and a social level; innocent women are accused of zina and brand-new marriages are destroyed on this false basis, which completely ignores the biological reality that not all women bleed upon their first sexual experience.

The practice of demanding and displaying vaginal blood as proof of virginity upon consummation of a marriage has no place in the Shari'ah. It is a practice of Jahiliyyah – pre-Islamic ignorance - and should be spoken against and abolished completely. Instead, we as an Ummah must return to the pure and holistic sexual ethics of our Deen, upholding the Sunnah, and not adopting and perpetuating warped mentalities and practices that damage our families and societies as a whole.

Zainab bint Younus is a Canadian Muslim woman who has been writing about social issues in the Ummah and female Islamic history for over ten years. As a founding member of MuslimMatters.org, she went on to write for SISTERS Magazine, AboutIslam.net, and other publications online. Currently on sabbatical from social media, she can be found at her blog: http://phoenixfaithandfire.blogspot.com

POST-NIKKAH, PRE-RUKHSATI: IS SEX ALLOWED?

By By Shaykh Yaser Birjas

Question:

I just had my nikkah done with my husband and we are having our rukhsati done soon in the next few months. The reason for the delay is just mainly to prepare for the wedding and to accommodate family members' schedule for the wedding. After the nikkah is it permissible to do all the acts that are permissible between a husband and wife even if the rukhsati hasn't been done?

Sincerely,
Getting married in my 20s

Answer:

From a technical Fiqhi perspective, when a man and woman have completed their *nikāḥ,* kitab or marriage contract [these are different terms for the same practice] they are Islamically considered to be husband and wife. It is permissible to delay the consummation of marriage (rukhsati or wedding) for a later and more convenient date with no specific time limit as long as they both mutually agree on it until the circumstances are right for them.

During this period between the nikāḥ and the rukhsati, it is permissible for the couple to interact with each other in a manner that is permissible for husband and wife, including the actual consummation of marriage.

However, if they do choose to be intimate with each other then the full rights of the wife become due upon the husband such as the full dowry and her right for housing and sustenance. What constitutes consummation of marriage is an issue of minor dispute among scholars. They all agree that having intercourse is a perfect definition but then some scholars say a perfect privacy is enough and others say being physically intimate in a manner less than actual intercourse is the minimum.

Having said that, some of the Fiqh rulings of non-devotional practices - such as marriage -are subject to cultural considerations. Hence, what is acceptable during that period between the nikāḥ and the rukhsati is subject to the general culture, the culture of both families and the actual agreement between the two contracting parties. Therefore, if the general culture entails the absolute abstinence during that period then this should be respected.

The young couple should respect the unpronounced stipulations that are in accordance with the cultural norms provided that these cultural norms don't violate any established principle of Fiqh.

Parents and the families of the two contracting parties expect the young couple to be at the level of maturity to adhere to these cultural norms. To bring the fitnah in the streets as an excuse to break these rules is not really a legitimate excuse and it could backfire. It's better to show a high standard of character even during those beautiful moments before officially moving in together.

Nevertheless, if the husband and wife do get intimate in the relationship prior to the official consummation of marriage they have not committed haram or sin, but it might cause some bitterness within the family because they might perceive it as disrespectful behavior. Therefore, it is definitely preferable to wait until the actual wedding date before the young couple can fully consummate the marriage.

May Allah give you all happiness, love and mercy. And Allah knows best.

Sh. Yaser Birjas received his Bachelors degree from Islamic University of Madinah in 1996 in Fiqh & Usool, graduating as the class valedictorian. After graduating, he went on to work as a youth counselor and relief program aide in war-torn Bosnia. Thereafter, he immigrated to the U.S. and currently resides in Dallas, Texas. He is also an instructor at AlMaghrib Institute, where he teaches popular seminars such as Fiqh of Love, The Code Evolved, and Heavenly Hues.

THE SEXLESS MUSLIM MARRIAGE

By Umm Ayoob

It is any woman's worst nightmare to find out that her husband is not attracted to her. It so happens that I am that woman. I am in an intimacy-starved marriage with my Muslim husband and have stayed in the marriage for 10 years. To be "intimacy-starved" means that we as a couple lack intimacy in terms of touch (something my husband dislikes), kissing (which does not appeal to him), and sex.

The Husband

From my description, you may understandably assume that my husband is a loner who is shy and asocial. However, quite the contrary is true. He is a charming, charismatic person, active in the Muslim community, and widely respected both at work and among his brethren for his integrity, hard work, and vision. I am very proud of him.

The Wife

With this, people may assume a number of things about my appearance and personality or situation. I will be brief by saying that everyone has personal preferences regarding looks. However, my husband chose me for marriage, knowing how I look and I didn't feel that he was being charitable in asking for my hand. I have a postgraduate degree, speak several languages and I would describe myself as flawed as anyone, but not generally unappealing.

So how did we get here?

We were young when we got married and this was the first relationship for both of us. We were (and still are) best friends. We laugh and have similar worldviews and goals. I love him and I have no doubts that he loves me. Our culture encourages spouses to remain married, so divorce wasn't an option I had initially considered. And why would I leave him? I loved him intensely and still do. However, intimate moments steadily declined.

I initially blamed it on the stress of living independently and his long working hours. Weeks turned into months and I tried reasoning with him. I asked him what was wrong and if I could change something; he eventually opened up about superficial matters. I took care of them, but that changed nothing. I explained a woman's need for feeling loved. I cited studies and explained chemicals released during the interaction that promote good feelings, but to no effect. I tried to seduce him and was rejected. I encouraged him to come with me to couples counseling without success. And when all else failed, I made *dua'a*.

Months turned into years and the problem persisted. I started to blame myself. I wasn't beautiful enough, thin enough, appealing enough. All of my insecurities were at full throttle. My self-esteem tapered off until nothing was left. Who would want me anyway?

I stayed in a dead end job because, although I had a postgraduate degree, I didn't consider myself smart enough to move ahead in a career. My depression, a diagnosis that had previously been mild, became severe. I was sick all the time. I had thoughts of killing myself.

My husband and I still enjoyed each other's company but I was noticeably miserable. My husband became upset at me for being miserable, and asked me to cheer up. I was lacking in everything including social upkeep, home upkeep, exercise routines, career moves, you name it. I threatened to leave him over this issue and formally asked for a divorce once. I went back on my own word however because I couldn't imagine my life without him; I loved him deeply and couldn't let go of the connection.

I was in the process of grieving and I didn't know it. I grieved the life I wish I had. I grieved at my own inadequacy of not being enough for him. My heart was broken and to a large extent, still is.

Why am I telling this story?

You may experience a difficulty and not realize how much it is affecting your life. The well-known sources of grief and difficulty in our communities include, among others: death, child concerns, handicap, financial worries and health problems. It is, to a large extent, societally acceptable to discuss these matters and highlight their hardship. However, I have never seen a sheikh, or a learned religious person publicly speak about my experience or the idea that gender stereotypes aren't always accurate. Lack of intimacy is an intensely private matter and likewise, an intense source of grief.

I have written this article in the hopes that others may realize the enormity of this issue and identify how harmful it is. I also wish that we would realize that stereotypes of any gender, including the sexuality of men aren't always true.

In my case, believing the stereotype that all men are extremely sexually inclined damaged me extensively because I expected my husband to display those tendencies, and when he didn't, I believed that something was wrong with me. I cannot lie and say that I feel adequate, even 10 years later. I haven't figured out my way yet.

If you are a woman finding yourself in my situation, let me reassure you: what is happening to you is not exclusive to you. Many women struggled silently with this issue. Shame has prevented many from speaking out or even seeking counsel from others.

It is most assuredly a difficult test, and with difficulties, *shaitaan* is ever present. You will be tempted. If you have not decided where your relationship is headed and are "waiting it out," several things may happen. You may want to start looking more attractive when you go out.

You may look things up on the internet to satisfy your urges, or even look for sexual outlets such as an affair. I am suggesting that this could happen to the most pious and proper of people.

Therefore, I advise you, my sister, to make a decision about your relationship for the sake of your *deen*. You have two options. Either you will decide to leave the relationship, or like me (for now), decide to stay.

In either case, I strongly suggest that you seek religious and psychological counseling. Counseling will help you deal with your emotions. It will also help you identify what intimacy actually means to you, and help you decide (with guidance) if it is something that you can live without.

From personal experience, your counselor does not need to be a Muslim to be able to help you. If your husband is willing to come with you, I would strongly suggest couples' counseling. From a religious point-of-view, know that if you decide to leave, this circumstance warrants the rights to a divorce, or a *khula'*. Consult with the imam of your community to arrange this.

If you choose to stay, you are certainly not alone in your decision. In this situation, it is essential that you continuously nurture your connection with Allah. Remind yourself that this life is temporary. Live your life solely for Allah, and He will help you throughout your difficulties. Become active in other areas of your life and do your best to excel in them. This will give your life meaning as well as give your self-esteem a boost. I ask Allah to strengthen you as He strengthened the Prophet Ayoob in his intense difficulties.

Allah is the Most Merciful, and verily with hardship there is relief.

Umm Ayoob is the pen-name of a sister who shared with us her private struggle, but asked that her public identity be withheld. Please make dua for her and for all those struggling with the challenges of intimacy in marriage.

THE SEXUAL WISDOM OF THE HADITH OF JABIR

By Dr. Yasir Qadhi

Jabir b. Abdillah is one of the most famous Companions of the Prophet ﷺ. He was from the Ansar, and accepted Islam as a young boy. He was also blessed to live an extremely long life. Because of this, Jabir became one of the most profuse narrators of hadith, earning his name in the top five Companions in terms of quantity of hadith narrated.

Jabir married young – he was probably seventeen or eighteen at the time, and his story is mentioned in most books of hadith, including the two *Sahihs*. It is a story that tells us much about how Islam views sexuality.

The hadith is as follows:

> Jabir b. Abdillah reported that once he was on an expedition with the Prophet ﷺ, and when they were close to the city of Madinah, he sped on his mount. The

41

Prophet ﷺ asked him why he was in such a hurry to return home.

Jabir replied, "I am recently married!"

The Prophet ﷺ asked, "To an older lady or a younger one?" [the Arabic could also read: "To a widow or a virgin?"], to which he replied, "A widow."

The Prophet ﷺ said, "But why didn't you marry a younger girl, so that you could play with her, and she could play with you, and you could make her laugh, and she could make you laugh?"

He said, "O Messenger of Allah! My father died a martyr at Uhud, leaving behind daughters, so I did not wish to marry a young girl like them, but rather an older one who could take care of them and look after them."

The Prophet ﷺ replied, "You have made the correct choice."

Jabir continued, "So when we were about to enter the city, the Prophet ﷺ said to me, 'Slow down, and enter at night, so that she who has not combed may comb her hair, and she who has not shaved may shave her private area.' Then he said to me, 'When you enter upon her, then be wise and gentle.'"

[Reported by al-Bukhari and Muslim, with various wordings, in their two Sahihs]

This is only part of a much larger hadith, known, not surprisingly, as the 'Hadith of Jabir'. It is a hadith full of benefits, and in fact separate treatises have been written by our scholars just on this one hadith. In this article, we are concerned with how this hadith sheds light on intimacy and marriage in Islam.

What first strikes us is the frankness of the Prophet's ﷺ question. He is encouraging Jabir to find a playful wife, and wants the both of them to enjoy each other. Clearly, the words of 'playfulness' and 'laughter' indicate that what is being encouraged is the couple's romance, foreplay and, generally, 'having fun' with one another.

This shows that it is one of the primary goals of a marriage that each party find satisfaction in the other. The connotation of being sexually playful is clearly implied, without any direct reference. From this, and many other references, we see that the Quran and Sunnah are frank about sexuality, but never vulgar. This should be our attitude and tone as well. It would do us well to contrast this straightforwardness of our Prophet with the ultra-reserved Muslim culture that we find around us, where even the words 'love' and 'romance' are considered filthy and are never be uttered in public.

Also, the Prophet ﷺ explicitly mentioned that *both* parties should be satisfied with each other ('…so that you may play with her and she may play with you…'). In most Muslim cultures, women's sexuality is sidelined or even suppressed. Not only is a woman's sexual feelings ignored, some cultures even cut off a part of a woman's sexual organ in order to minimize her sexuality through barbaric practices such as FGM – female genital mutilation.

A woman's sexuality is no less important than a man's, and it is essential that a woman also be given her due right.

One phrase in this hadith that many men concentrate on is the encouragement to Jabir that he should marry a young woman. However, they ignore the context of the hadith and also the response of the Prophet ﷺ. Jabir himself was a young man, and that is why he was asked why he would marry an older lady. Typically, a young man marries a young lady.

When Jabir gave a legitimate reason for choosing an older lady, he was informed that he had, in fact, made the *correct* decision. One should always remember that even our Prophet first married Khadija, a lady senior to him in age, and remained with her for all of her life. Khadija was the most beloved wife of our Prophet, and even Aisha could not compete against that love.

The command to Jabir not to enter the city until nightfall was because the Prophet ﷺ did not want Jabir to surprise his wife. At a time when there were no cell phones or other means of informing the family when a traveler would return, the Prophet ﷺ would send a crier into the city, announcing that the caravan was returning. The crier would alert the inhabitants of the city (including Jabir's wife), and they would then prepare themselves to great the returning travelers. Hence, he told Jabir to wait for this crier before proceeding into the city.

From this, we learn that spouses should physically beautify themselves for one another. Combing the hair is one way to beautify; anything that increases the beauty and handsomeness of one spouse in front of the other is something to be encouraged. The Prophet ﷺ told the impatient Jabir that it was better for him to delay his arrival in order that his wife could prepare herself for him.

The explicit command to shave the pubic area is an amazing phrase. We all know that a part of our Islamic tradition is that one must shave one's pubic area; in this tradition, this command is put in the context of the sexual act.

In other words, the husband is told to be patient so that his wife may beautify her private area in order to increase the aesthetic pleasure and gratification of sex. A husband and wife *should* make sure that even around their private areas, they look attractive to each other. Again and again, we see the frankness of the prophetic traditions and contrast this to the ultra-conservative attitudes predominant in many Muslim cultures.

Some people erroneously believe that a husband and wife should never look at each other's private area. This belief is not based upon any authentic textual evidence – in fact, there are numerous evidences (including this one) that clearly state otherwise. If a husband will not enjoy the body of his wife, who else will he enjoy? The same applies for a woman with her husband's body.

The last phrase of the hadith is translated as '…then be wise and gentle'. The Arabic is '*fa-l-kayyis al-kayyis*', or, in another wording, '*zafar al-kayyis*.' The word '*kayyis*' primarily means wisdom, but it also has the connotation of gentleness. Scholars have understood this phrase to be an indirect reference that Jabir should approach his wife in a gentle and 'wise' manner.

Imam al-Bukhari, Ibn Khuzaymah, and Ibn Hibban all narrated this wording, and they all understood the reference here to be an indirect reference to the sexual act. Once again, the wording is frank without being vulgar. What is meant by '*al-kayyis*' is that Jabir should act in a wise manner; he has been gone for some time, and is newly married. Therefore, both parties are missing each other, and it is a sign of wisdom that they gratify themselves and do not delay this unnecessarily.

Also, there is a connotation of gentleness as well; Jabir should realize that he is a young man, and therefore he should not act in a manner that might be painful to his wife. The fact that the Prophet ﷺ is instructing Jabir what to do at this time shows that he instructed his Ummah even about such personal matters.

In one hadith, which deals with the etiquette of the restroom, the Prophet ﷺ said, "I am to you like a father, I teach you [what you need to know]…" [Reported by Abu Dawud].

Since Jabir did not have any older brothers, and his father had passed away, the Prophet ﷺ took on this responsibility, and even advised him about sexual conduct. From this, we may extrapolate that people of knowledge, or elders of the community, should likewise not be shy when it comes to teaching Muslims about sexual etiquette.

The Islamic attitude towards sex is completely at odds with those of many Christian thinkers. St. Augustine, who is perhaps the single most influential theologian of early Christianity, viewed sexual desire as something 'foul' to be guilty and ashamed of.

His writings had a profound impact on all future Christian notions of sex, and were also used to justify the prohibition of priests getting married. That is why, to this day, even many non-religious Christians are baffled by Islam's attitude towards sex. It is mainly due to such notions that Islam has been viewed by many Westerners as being a 'licentious' religion.

Such hadiths like this one of Jabir are mocked and ridiculed. One website I read commented, "How can a prophet of God command his followers to enjoy their wives?"

This shock stems from the basic Augustinian notion of sex being inherently evil. We must be aware of these psychological underpinnings when discussing Islam with others. For us as Muslims, sexual desire in and of itself is *never* associated with evil; it is only the misuse and abuse of such desire that is evil. Rather, quite the contrary, sex is quite clearly implied in the Quran as being a blessing from Allah, to be thoroughly enjoyed between spouses.

There are many evidences that clearly demonstrate Islam's realistic and pragmatic view of human sexuality. Sexuality, like all human emotions, is a natural instinct that should be satisfied in a permissible manner. The emotion itself is not evil or filthy; abusing it and trying to satisfy it outside of the permissible bounds of marriage is evil and filthy.

The Prophet ﷺ himself said, "From this world, women and perfume have been made beloved to me, but the coolness of my eye comes from prayer" [al-Bukhari].

And in the famous hadith, he also said, "This whole world is an enjoyment, and its best enjoyment is a righteous wife" [Muslim].

A righteous wife, and by analogy a righteous husband, is the best *enjoyment* of this world. Pure, *halal*, encouraged *enjoyment*.

In another tradition, we are advised "If one of you approaches his wife, and then wishes to repeat, let him do *wudhu*, for it will make the recurrence more energetic" [Abu Dawud].

In all of these hadiths, we see once again the clear *encouragement* to engage in passionate and fulfilling sex with one's spouse. The frank advice given makes it crystal clear that we should aim to have healthy sex lives. No less a figure than our beloved Prophet informed us of ways to increase our love and make the act of intimacy more fulfilling. Washing oneself after a first act invigorates the body and rejuvenates the soul, and thus helps in repeating the act again.

What is truly amazing is that while the message is crystal clear in each and every one of these traditions, never is the wording vulgar, nor is the language crude. Similarly, we should be frank in our teachings, but there is no need to employ unbefitting language.

Let us conclude this article by mentioning a quote from one of the most famous medieval scholars of our religion. Imam al-Ghazali (d. 505) mentions in his famous work *The Revival of the Religious Sciences* that scholars have mentioned many blessings of sex, such as protecting one's chastity and increasing one's progeny. But he also mentions a blessing that might surprise many Muslims. One of the blessings of sex that our scholars have mentioned, al-Ghazali says, is to experience some of the pleasures of the afterlife. He continues:

"**And I swear, what they have said is absolutely true! For indeed, in this pleasure [of sex] – a pleasure that cannot be compared to *any* other pleasure – if only it were to persist, it would indeed be a sign or signal for those pleasures of the next life that have been promised to us.**

To entice someone regarding a pleasure that he has never experienced is of no use! If an impotent man were to be enticed with sex, or a young child with power, there would be no temptation. Therefore, one of the blessings of the sexual experience and pleasure in this world is the hope of its perpetual existence in the next, so that this can be used as a motivation for the worship of Allah.

Marvel, therefore, at the wisdom of Allah, and His Mercy, for look at how He has placed in one desire two lives: an external life, and an internal life. So the external life is the preservation of a man through his progeny and children. And the internal life is the life of the next world. For the pleasure of sex is diminished

in this world because it must remain temporary, and is swiftly terminated, but by experiencing it, one's desire to have such a pleasure remain everlasting becomes firm, and this encourages one to persist in deeds of worship that would allow him to experience such pleasures."

Sh. Dr. Yasir Qadhi has a Bachelors in Hadith and a Masters in Theology from Islamic University of Madinah, and a PhD in Islamic Studies from Yale University. He is currently the Dean of Academic Affairs at The Islamic Seminary of America.

OVERCOMING MASTURBATION

By Haleh Banani

Question:

I want to ask this: will Allah pardon my sins even if I repeat it again and again after a *tawbah*? I also want to let you know that since the day I was born (as a Muslim) I was never interested in fully applying, practicing or studying Islam until 2011 when I really felt the emptiness in me, so I don't really understands Islam YET. My situation is that I've been struggling to stop my masturbating addiction.

Once I stopped for a week, then did it again. Feeling guilty, then I stopped again and did it once or twice in another week. I stayed like this for around 4 or 5 months since the day I decided to stop masturbating. I know that masturbating (self-sex, etc) is Haram/forbidden and has no good… I really, really wanted to stop, but it's so hard. What I fear the most is the thought that Allah has locked my heart and put me way from the Right Path, sirat'l-mustaqim.

Answer:

First, I would like to commend you for recognizing your shortcoming and seeking help. It's not easy to admit when you have a weakness – it actually takes a lot of strength.

With the number of people writing in and asking about this same issue I want you to know that YOU ARE NOT ALONE. Many people suffer silently due to their addiction to masturbation. The fact that you have been able to stop it for 4-5 months is very good progress masha'Allah. In order to take control of this habit completely you need to make certain adjustments.

Create Motivation to Change

Everything that you do is driven by one of 2 principles: to seek pleasure or to avoid pain. Therefore; you need to link as much pain as you can to the behavior that you want to end (masturbation). Ask yourself:

> What will it cost you as far your self-esteem, spirituality and self-control if you were to give in to your addiction?

> How will it negatively affect your relationships either now or in the future?

> How will you feel about yourself if you succumb to your lust?

As you reflect on the answers to these questions, you will start creating a negative association to the act. The stronger the emotions, the more effective it will be.

Then, you need to create positive associations to your desired goal: stopping the masturbation. Ask yourself this:

> How you will feel about yourself if you demonstrate self-control & self-leadership?

> How will you feel spiritually, knowing that you are giving up your lust for the sake of Allah?

> How will your relationships improve once you are no longer addicted?

> Reflecting on all the benefits of stopping will increase your self-control and motivation.

Understand the Addiction

On a physiological level, the mind becomes easily addicted to the epinephrine (Adrenaline) and serotonin that is released during sexual arousal and orgasm. It is as addictive as heroine.

With each act, the addiction becomes stronger and stronger until masturbation is not only as a means of satisfying sexual curiosity, but also as an outlet for other emotions such as boredom, anxiety, fear and loneliness.

This is when it can totally take over your life, since it becomes your first line of defense in alleviating negative emotions.

It's important to realize that the strong craving that you have, like many other physiological impulses, are shaped like a bell curve. You need to learn to ride out the craving because it is not going to last forever. If you wait long enough the craving will go away and you will gain control over your impulses. This is easier said than done, but with enough persistence & positive conditioning it is possible.

You can also take some practical steps to reduce the risk of facing, or succumbing to the urge.

1. Avoid loneliness & boredom
2. Keep yourself busy
3. Stay proactive by volunteering your time
4. Exert your energy through exercise
5. Seek the company of righteous friends that can be a positive influence on you and your iman.
6. Put a content filter on your computer with a complicated override password that you have to look up (or have your friend set the password) and have the history of your searches sent to a trusted, respected friend who can support you through accountability.
7. Avoid watching or listening to anything sexual
8. Pray to Allah to strengthen you

Spiritual Strength

Know that regardless of the mistakes you make, the door of repentance is always open and Allah is all Forgiving. The fact that you are striving to improve yourself is admirable and Allah not only sees your struggle but rewards you each time you control your impulses.

Think the best of Allah and be sure that He would not seal your heart when you are striving to be better. Strengthen your bond with Allah by praying and asking Him to remove this addiction and help you to overcome your weakness. I pray that you can keep your new commitment to Allah knowing that He will not abandon you just because you get weak from time to time.

Haleh Banani has a Master's degree in Clinical Psychology with 20 years of experience working with couples and individuals. She was a featured expert on Al-Jazeera international, Huda TV, Islamic Open University, Mercy Mission and Bayinnah TV. Haleh is an instructor for Ilmflix and Qalam Institute. She is an international speaker and writer.

CONFRONTING SEX ADDICTION IN THE MUSLIM COMMUNITY

By Abeda Ahmed

This brother in his 60s - with a beard and jubbah - sat in front of me with his head hung down and hands clasped firmly together. His knuckles were turning white from the pressure. I could see that talking about his issue was draining and it was taking every ounce of courage and willpower for him to do so.

He said he knew it was wrong. He felt devastated and guilt-ridden after each episode. He had huge regrets for the sadness he had brought to his marriage, but he felt he just couldn't stop acting out. He was regular in his prayers, righteous in performing his other Islamic duties, volunteered at the local charitable causes and by all means was a law abiding and extremely humble and mellow mannered individual.

This brother had an addiction to watching pornography and he had, along with his wife, suffered for over 30 years in a cycle of compulsion, secrets, shame, frustration, guilt, hopelessness, worthlessness and inevitable isolation.

Sex and porn addiction is a real problem and just like drugs and alcohol, this pandemic has secretly and slowly permeated the Muslim community too. In the United States an estimated 30 million individuals are struggling with sex addiction. This includes out of control sexual behaviors like compulsive use of pornography, visiting sex workers, using adult hook-up apps, or having multiple affairs.

Neuroscientists believe that the changes in the brain of the sex addict are the same seen in a drug addict. Dopamine is the common denominator in all addictions.

With an estimated 1.7 billion active users on Facebook alone, 90% of 16-24 year olds in the western world own a smartphone. In a recent study carried out by the NSPCC of 1,000 children aged 11-16, 94% admitted they had been exposed to pornography by the age of 14. Porn is a 97 million dollar industry- worth more than Apple, Google, Netflix, yahoo combined.

Although at present, we don't have any specific statistics for Muslims, it is an increasing presentation in in my therapy experience. It is a real problem and we cannot minimize it or just leave it to the individual's spiritual growth and ability to abstain and refrain.

Remember, for a long time we Muslims had the same attitude towards mental health issues where we linked depression and anxiety to lack of faith and lack of patience. This meant many people struggled and suffered in silence, not knowing that depression is an illness needing treatment, sometimes with medication, psychological intervention, or both.

Alhamdulillah, we have made progress with mental health and I hope Insha'Allah we can do the same for sexual addiction. When we acknowledge that it becomes an addictive compulsion, not a choice, it will give people who are suffering the courage and permission to speak and seek help.

My model of working with individuals who struggle with sex addiction is to use the core therapeutic skills of being compassionate and non-judgmental, so that a neutral platform is provided where the addict can come for help.

Allah told his Beloved Prophet ﷺ "so by mercy from Allah, [O Muhammad], you were lenient with them. And if you had been rude [in speech] and harsh in heart, they would have disbanded from about you. So pardon them and ask forgiveness for them and consult them in the matter. And when you have decided, then rely upon Allah. Indeed, Allah loves those who rely [upon Him] (3:159)

Spiritual, emotional and psychological healing comes hand in hand during therapy and as gradually the shame and hopelessness is reduced, the client begins to connect again with the true concept of Allah's Mercy and instead of shame — which mocks and rebukes, making the person feel inadequate.

We work on connecting with self-reflection and remorse so gradually an inner accountability is developed. Treatment is based on developing new habits based on surrender, gratitude, renewed spiritual connection and establishing and re-establishing meaningful relationships.

Sex addiction festers in darkness. People go about their "normal" lives by day, but the claws of compulsion leave them surrendering to their desires by night. Coupled with the deep-rooted belief that they are doomed to hell, sex-addicts fall into a trap from Shaytan. A sex addict starts recovering when he or she moves from a place of darkness to light and hope. Healing comes when body, mind and heart are all seeking the same thing, so the focus of the therapy is to work on all three areas.

Sex addiction is a sin. It may not be a crime by the law of the countries we reside in but it is a sin. But who said there is no hope for sinners? We all know the story of the prostitute who was given the glad tidings of Jannah because of her charitable act of kindness of giving water to a thirsty dog!

> **Like all sinners, the sex addict needs to painfully unlearn old habits, to dismantle old scenarios, to pay old debts, and then to move steadfastly along the road to recovery one small, secure step at a time. (Hall, 2016)**

Our imams and scholars need to use their platforms to talk about this issue to help raise awareness, and to help us create support structures for those who are struggling. The treatment model is based on understanding where the issue stems from and giving strategies which work for the individual in recovery and to provide relapse prevention.

With Allah's mercy and guidance, our bearded brother in the jubbah completed a year of regular therapy. As a child, he had been sexually abused from the age of 6. He also witnessed a lot of physical abuse directed towards his mother by his father and was bullied throughout school.

This brother's addiction was trauma and attachment induced, and throughout his life his way of dealing with his painful memories and lack of assertiveness and confidence was to use porn as an anesthetizing tool. I worked with him by addressing his childhood issues and by giving those wounds a closure and slowly building his confidence and self-esteem. We used relapse prevention techniques and introduced a deeper understanding of triggers and how a sustainable sense of accountability to Allah, himself and family. He finally broke the cycle of addiction and managed to begin repairing his relationship with Allah, himself, his wife and his children.

Abeda Ahmed is a qualified therapist based in Birmingham who specializes in relationship issues and is also sex addiction therapist who works with Muslim clients. You can contact her on info@amanahcoun-selling.com

FROM A SAME-SEX ATTRACTED MUSLIM: BETWEEN DENIAL OF REALITY AND DISTORTION OF RELIGION

By Brother Yusuf

In the late 1990s, one of North America's most prominent Muslim leaders was giving a lecture at a large convention. In that lecture, he described how disgusted he was that he had been sitting next to a gay man on his flight over to the lecture. An 18-year-old Muslim experiencing same-sex attractions was at that lecture, and the words like raining bullets are stuck in my head till this day.

Let me introduce myself. My name is Yousef and I write to you as a Muslim who has experienced same-sex attractions since adolescence. I am currently married with children, *al-hamdu li'Llah*, and have been working for many years now as a professional.

My same-sex attractions, while still present, have diminished significantly over the years, and I have been blessed to enjoy a healthy relationship with my wife, whom I love. (As a side note, while marriage was definitely the right decision for me, it may not be right for every person who has same-sex attractions; no single rule applies to all situations.) I have also been the moderator of an online support group for Muslims with same-sex desires, called Straight Struggle, for about 13 years now. In that time, I have transformed, grown, and evolved in my thinking many times over, specifically with regard to the topic of homosexuality and Islam.

Critical Terms and Concepts

I will be using two main terms in this essay: same-sex attractions (SSA) and same-sex encounters (SSE). I believe these terms more accurately describe the relevant issues with respect to the topic of homosexuality, particularly for us as Muslims. The terms "homosexual," "gay," "LGBT," "queer," etc. in today's culture are labels that mean different things to different people, whereas there is no mistaking what is meant by "same-sex attractions / desires" and "same-sex encounters."

It is also important for me to stress that I do not believe that my same-sex attractions are my identity. Same-sex desires are feelings that I, and others, have that I contend with in my daily journey towards Allah. They do not make me different in any essential way from any other Muslim. For this reason, I reject the idea that Muslims who experience same-sex attractions should be given a special label or that we should "self-identify" as "LBGT," "gay," "homosexual," or "queer." I believe these labels isolate people with such attractions and, from what I have seen, sometimes force them to conform to certain lifestyles even if they do not really want to. Also, these labels have the effect of elevating sexual desires – basically *shahawat* – and making them part of the "core of who I am" as a person. This seems arbitrary to me and something that I find hard to justify from an Islamic perspective, both legally and spiritually.

To be clear and upfront: there is absolutely nothing *haram* or to be ridiculed about anyone just having SSA (same-sex attractions). What is forbidden in Islam are SSEs (same-sex encounters and behaviors). No one that I have met over the years ever chose to be attracted to the same sex. Let me repeat: not one single person among the dozens and dozens that I have interacted with over the years ever wanted to have SSA or chose to have SSA. This needs to be understood and taken into account when thinking about your brothers and sisters who are dealing with this issue.

It is also critical that people in the Muslim community understand that there is a very important difference between SSA and SSE, between *attractions* and *actions*. Practically all of our religion rides on this distinction, not just in the sexual realm but across the board. I am not judged for merely experiencing a desire (to the extent that it is beyond my control), but only for what I choose to do – or not to do – with it. A person is not cursed or diseased or a walking sin just because they experience SSA. Only an action can be *haram*, not a person. Rather, they are people just like anyone else who are dealing with a particular difficulty or test in life, and they are doing the best they can with their life and faith. They have failures and successes just like everyone else. Of course, if we apply the distinction between desires and actions consistently, then we who experience SSA also have to concede that just because we have these desires – which can be very strong, as sexual desires often are – this does not justify us acting on them in defiance of Allah's command.

Who Are Your Brothers and Sisters That Struggle with SSA?

I have thought long and hard about what to write in this essay and it has been something that, in some ways, has been years in the making. I thought I might proceed by giving you some examples of the brothers and sisters that I have encountered over the years. I could tell you about the brother who, from a very young age until he was a young adult, was sexually abused by his older neighbor. I could tell you about the guilt he had since the abuse "felt good" at the time, along with the attention. Or maybe I can tell you about the brother who attempted suicide twice since his family found out about his SSA. Or the sister who lost her job because of rumors about her SSA. Or the brothers who contracted HIV as a result of SSEs.

On the other hand, I could tell you about the imam who chose his faith over his desires and continues to preach, practice, and live as a pious Muslim on his path towards Allah even while keeping his desires in check. Or the community leader who chose a life of celibacy while learning and teaching the faith to others. Or the man who was living a homosexual lifestyle with his partner and who left it all for the sake of Allah when he converted to Islam. Or the number of university professors and doctors and other professionals who made the conscious decision to defeat their *nafs* and who chose Allah above all else in order to attain the ultimate reward. These brothers and sisters, myself included, firmly reject the idea of making religion conform to one's needs and desires and rather struggle against themselves in order to follow the teachings of our faith.

What Causes SSA and Can It Be Changed?

The question sometimes comes up as to what causes a person to have SSA. There has been a lot of discussion and research on this issue, and the fact is that no one really knows. It seems that it is most likely due to many convergent factors that are different for each person. Also, the exact nature and intensity of one's SSA can vary from person to person. I have learned through my long experience that no two people's profiles are exactly the same.

Some people with SSA experience attraction to their own sex as a rule but are not positively repulsed by the other sex. Some of these might be able to see themselves with an opposite-gender spouse one day, if the right person and conditions came along and they had their SSA firmly under control, were confident they wouldn't fall into SSEs while married, etc. This, in fact, has been my experience and that of a number of others I have known. Other people have no attraction toward the opposite sex at all and may even cringe at the thought of engaging them romantically. Conventional marriage, needless to say, would not be an advisable option for such a person, at least as long as this remains their state.

Also, some people really feel a need to "get to the bottom of" their SSA, to try to understand it and figure it out: what it is, where it came from, why it's there, what it "means." Others don't care much how it got there or why they have it, but prefer just to focus instead on how to manage it effectively and get on with their lives. Personally, I have come to belong more to this second camp.

When I was younger, I did spend time trying to figure out why I was this way or what "went wrong." Eventually I stopped because I figured I didn't really need to know the "why" of it, but rather just the "how" of how to deal with it. And even this "how" is not something I can explain in any scientific way. It is just things that have worked out for me over the years – mostly through following the Sunna, learning how to outsmart my *nafs* through the practice of *tazkiya*, and a fair amount of good old trial and error.

All this raises another common question, namely, can SSA be "cured"? If "cure" means total elimination and 100% "heterosexuality," then probably not. Statistically, it seems uncommon for someone who has experienced predominant or exclusive same-sex attractions consistently past the age of adolescence one day to have zero SSA susceptibilities and to become fully "heterosexual." But this goal isn't just unattainable (for most); I also believe that it is unnecessary.

Nothing in Islam says that I have to be "heterosexual," in fact, we don't even have a word for that in our *deen*. Islam says only that I must refrain from prohibited sexual *acts*, which *are* named and specified in our *deen*. Past scholars, for example, differed over whether it was blameworthy for a mature man to be enticed by the beauty of a younger male (typically a "beardless youth," or *amrad*). Some thought that such susceptibilities were indeed blameworthy, but many apparently did not – as long as no *haram* actions were committed.

This last point about avoiding *haram* actions has been agreed upon by all Muslim scholars. This is why it is so important for us to keep in mind the distinction between desires and actions. As Muslims, we know that Allah [swt] will ask us about what He has put under our control. This always includes our actions, as well as our thoughts and fantasies *to the extent that* we have control over them. *Taklif* (moral accountability) would be meaningless if Allah had not given us jurisdiction over our actions and made us fully responsible for them. Of course we will all mess up and make numerous mistakes along the way, whether we are people who happen to be tested with same-sex desires or not. This is exactly what Allah has made *tawba* (repentance) for.

It is also why Allah refers to Himself eight times in the Qur'an as "*al-Tawwab al-Rahim*," the Merciful One

Who ever turns back to His repenting servant, and assures us no fewer than *72* times (!) that He is *"Ghafur(un) Rahim,"* the Ever Forgiving, Merciful One – *subhan Allah!* Therefore, no amount of sin should cause a person to lose hope in the Mercy of Allah. At the same time, our chances of receiving Allah's help, and earning His ultimate pleasure, are always greater when we minimize our sins as much as we can.

Coming back to the question of change, the fact remains that many people with SSA have experienced meaningful change over time in the intensity of their desires and the hold their same-sex attractions have over them, and/or in the role these desires and attractions play in their lives and their sense of who they are. Sometimes this may happen on its own. Sometimes it is the result of long-term spiritual discipline and self-control. Sometimes it's a question of changing how you conceive of and define yourself in relation to your desires and to others, particularly those of your own sex.

More often than not, any progress a person makes on the path of dealing with his or her SSA will usually come about through a combination of techniques and approaches. Some have benefited from professional, faith-friendly therapy in learning to understand and address their same-sex desires and related emotional and psychological issues that many people with SSA are often also struggling with. Others have reported benefiting greatly from books, programs, and resources meant specifically for addressing, comprehending, mastering, and reducing or minimizing one's SSA.

A wealth of useful, principled, and thought-provoking information – grounded in a Christian, but also a more generally religious, perspective that Muslims can derive benefit from as well – can be found, for example, at sites such as www.samesexattraction.org or www.peoplecanchange.com. But again for me, the real goal is not "heterosexuality" per se, but rather contentment, fulfillment, and being at peace with Allah, myself, and others.

Islam as a Middle Path: Avoiding Extreme Narratives

"I Am a Walking Monstrosity and Allah Hates Me for Existing" vs. "Out and Proud: It's Okay to Be Gay!"

I believe a key step in reaching equilibrium in the process of dealing with SSA is learning to avoid two common extremes: the extreme of despising ourselves for mere desires and attractions we did not ask for and the extreme of "identifying with" these desires as somehow defining who we are as human beings and as Muslims. Islam, as always, is a Middle Way, and it can be very liberating when we learn to get beyond all the false scripts we've been fed by our modern culture and to conceive of our particular moral struggle as no different in essence from the moral struggle of any other Muslim. When we do this, we can then learn to see ourselves as no worse, no better, nor even different in any fundamental way from any other sincerely striving servant of God on this planet.

We also reject any attempt on the part of anyone to pressure or to bully Muslim communities, imams, leaders, mosques, schools, or other institutions into accepting what Allah has clearly made *haram* in the name of "tolerance," "affirmation," "acceptance," "inclusion," "diversity," or any of the other buzz words that are normally used for this purpose.

This talk of extremes – which are always un-Islamic – brings me to another point. Many Muslims dealing with same-sex attractions find themselves stuck today between two sharply opposing forces. The first, which has been debated and now effectively refuted on the level of Islamic teachings (see <u>M. Vaid, "Can Islam Accommodate Homosexual Acts? Qur'anic Revisionism and the Case of Scott Kugle"</u>), are self-described "progressive Muslims" who have taken it upon themselves to offer distorted interpretations of the Qur'an and who reject or dismiss *ahadith* and the consensus of Muslim scholars, all in an attempt to make SSEs – same-sex acts, encounters, and relationships – permissible in Islam.

This group, however, is appealing to some because it offers a "safe space" for Muslims with SSA and offers them a lifestyle that they can easily identify with. Of course, the biggest drawback is that the life such Muslims would be leading is likely to be sinful in many ways. I feel I have to say it clearly here once again: I and many other same-sex attracted Muslims that I have encountered over the years completely reject such attempts to manipulate our religion in order to "accommodate" our (or anyone else's) "sexuality."

We also reject any attempt on the part of anyone to pressure or to bully Muslim communities, imams, leaders, mosques, schools, or other institutions into accepting what Allah has clearly made *haram* in the name of "tolerance," "affirmation," "acceptance," "inclusion," "diversity," or any of the other buzz words that are normally used for this purpose. The meaning of Islam is "submission," and my submission to Allah and my faith come above all else, including my own desires, sexual or otherwise. This is the test that Allah has chosen for me and I accept it from Him in hopes of attaining His pleasure and His reward, insha'Allah. Allah mentions in the Holy Qur'an in Surat al-Baqara (2), verses 155-157:

> *And We shall surely test you with something of fear and hunger and a loss of wealth and lives and fruits, but give good tidings to the patient, Who, when affliction strikes them, say, "Indeed we belong to Allah, and indeed to Him will we return." Those are the ones upon whom are blessings from their Lord and mercy. And it is those who are the [rightly] guided.*

According to the tafsir of this verse, these tribulations from Allah come in many forms that we have no control over. It is only Allah that can choose what these tribulations look like. The only control that we have is how we respond to them. Will we give in to temptation? Will we give up? Or will we persevere with patience and remind ourselves of our ultimate goal in the journey towards Allah? Then Allah can count us among the muhtadeen, the rightly guided who deserve Allah's blessings and mercy.

So how do we know that we will be tested even if we believe, and that tests and trials are actually proof that we do believe? In the Qur'an in Surat al-'Ankabut (29), verses 2-7, Allah says:

Do people think they shall be left to say, "We believe" and they shall not be tried? But We have certainly tried those before them, and Allah will surely make evident those who are truthful, and He will surely make evident the liars. Or do those who do evil deeds think they can out-run Us? Evil is what they judge. Whoever hopes for the meeting with Allah – indeed, the term decreed by Allah is coming. And He is the Hearing, the Knowing. And whoever strives only strives for [the benefit of] himself. Indeed, Allah is free from need of the worlds. And those who believe and do righteous deeds – We shall surely re-move from them their misdeeds and shall surely reward them according to the best of what they were wont to do.

These verses are very clear in their message that belief will be met with trials. Accepting that these are trials and striving against them for the sake of Allah is what is of utmost importance as a statement and proof of our faith, because ultimately it is Allah's meeting that we seek in the Hereafter no matter what hardship we face in this life on our path towards Him.

So, on the one side are people who try to distort the *deen* by changing its clear teachings, but then on the other side there is often the culture of hate and stigma within the Muslim community with respect to people who experience SSA: whether it be the fact that this topic is hardly ever discussed – leading Muslims dealing with it to find themselves in bubbles where many young people think that they are literally the only people in the world that could be dealing with it – or the fact that if the topic ever is "discussed," it is likely by imams who describe how "the punishment of homosexuality is death" and how evil the people of Lut [alayhis] were. Other ways it is "discussed" are with groups of friends who seem to find it okay to make fun of, ridicule, and put down "gays." Even for many of us who don't act on our same-sex desires and reject the notion of self-identifying as "gay," we still feel that people like us are being targeted by these kinds of comments.

In my many years, I can only recall twice when someone who spoke about the topic of homosexuality in Islam was actually compassionate and understanding enough to say that these are our brothers and sisters and they need our support and help. Twice is not enough. This needs to be the mainstream message that is presented the majority of the time to ensure that people get the correct understanding.

Our Responsibility as a Community

It is no longer – and really never should have been – acceptable that we sweep this issue under the rug. We are losing far too many of our brothers and sisters because of the ignorance of those in places of authority and the indifference and carelessness of the general community.

Where are the *khutba*s and *durus* where this topic is properly addressed and correctly presented so that people have the proper understanding of the issue from an Islamic perspective? Where are the imams and scholars explaining that the presence of a spontaneous desire is not sinful in and of itself and unpacking the amorphous categories of "homosexuality" and "LGBT" into the more concrete – and religiously faithful – distinction between SSAs and SSEs?

Where are the *khawatir* telling people to watch their tongues when speaking about "gays and lesbians" and "homosexuals" so as not to hurt the feelings of their brothers and sisters who are suffering in silence? Even as we reject these identity labels and caution the community against taking them over from secular culture.

Where is the research to allow parents properly to guide their children so they can come to them with such an issue? And where are the tools parents need to be able to help their children who do end up coming to them with the issue of SSA? Until we, the mainstream Muslim community, find a way to offer a safe environment for people dealing with same-sex attractions to open up to caring and compassionate individuals among us, we will be losing many of our brothers and sisters to a falsified understanding of Islam, or to leaving the religion altogether, or even to suicide (*wa'l-'iyadhu bi'Llah*).

Now, I certainly do not mean that people should start waving the rainbow flag, wearing pink triangles, and proclaiming their same-sex attractions publicly. What I do mean is that we need to end the isolation and misinformation about SSA. Imams and leaders need to propagate the correct understanding of same-sex attractions (SSA) versus same-sex encounters (SSE) in terms of *halal* and *haram*.

Imams, leaders, and parents must also acquire the tools necessary to be able to support their children if/when they disclose their SSA to them. If we cannot count on our leaders and our communities both to uphold the integrity of our faith and at the same time to support us – your brothers and sisters who are dealing with same-sex attractions – with wisdom, discretion, and compassion in this test that Allah has chosen for us, then who can we count on?

Please note that I am not asking for anyone's pity. What I am asking for is some compassion – true compassion rooted in proper Islamic teachings that ensure our welfare as Muslims both in this life and the next. When someone, especially a young person, hears things like "gays should be killed" or "gays are disgusting," I don't think one can exaggerate the lasting effects such words can have on a confused and vulnerable soul.

Many of our youth are leaving the *deen* over this issue, or going over to groups that "affirm" them – however misguidedly – in a gay identity and lifestyle. We as a community should feel sadness and a sense of culpability on both counts. But in addition to the true compassion of our Prophet [saw]– who was the most merciful of all mankind yet never compromised in warning people against violating the command of Allah – I am also asking for respect. It is my right as your brother in faith to have your full respect and support. This includes respect and support for brothers who might be effeminate in their behavior or sisters who might be masculine in theirs through no fault of their own. Imam al-Nawawi [ranhu] has stated, concerning a male with effeminate mannerisms (*mukhannath*):

> "The scholars have said that the *mukhannath* is of two types. The first is one who was created like that; he did not deliberately take on the characteristics of women, their appearance, speech, and mannerisms. Rather, this is a disposition (*khilqa*) upon which Allah created him. For this [person], there is no blame, no rebuke, no sin, and no penalty, and he is excused as he has no hand in that. The second type of *mukhannath* is the one who was not created upon that disposition (*khilqa*). Rather, he deliberately takes on the characteristics of women, their mannerisms, appearance, and speech, and adopts their dress. This is what is blameworthy and has been reported in authentic hadiths as cursed [behavior]. This accords with the meaning of another hadith: 'Allah has cursed men who (deliberately) imitate women, and women who (deliberately) imitate men.'"

Imam al-Nawawi is clear here that there is no blame on a person for such tendencies as they have little or no control over. (Scholars agree that a person whose mannerisms mismatch their biological sex should try to recondition their mannerisms to the degree possible, but that they are not blameworthy for what lies beyond their capacity in this domain.) So long as someone is not committing *haram* acts – and really, even if they are – they are still your brother or sister in faith and there is absolutely no justification for disrespecting or bullying them. As long as they are not trying to justify or to normalize any *haram* behaviors – like same-sex acts – or calling to them publicly, they should be accepted and treated just like anyone else.

Words of Advice to Fellow Muslims Dealing with SSA

In closing, I would like to offer some *nasiha* to my many brothers and sisters who read this that also deal, as I do, with unrequested same-sex desires. First of all, you should know that you are not alone. There are many of us out there just like you, who know exactly what you are going through – the confusion, the pain, the isolation. We are here to lean on and to support each other with helpful words of advice, an ear to listen, and brotherly/sisterly encouragement along what we know through experience can be a very difficult path.

Secondly, as all help and support ultimately come from Allah [swt], I cannot stress how critical it is to maintain one's relationship with the One Who created us, to trust in Him, and to remain as close to Him as possible – no matter how many times one may have messed up or fallen flat on one's face in managing one's sexual desires. Many factors are necessary in dealing effectively with SSA, as I have mentioned, but in my experience, the single most important overriding factor for me has been my faith in Allah,[swt] and my unwavering faith in and commitment to His *deen*. Without this critical element, I do not believe I would be anywhere near where I am today in all of this, *wa'l-hamdu li'Llah*.

Finally, I would like to point out that there is no "one path" on the struggle with same-sex desires, no single place that every individual will end up in this life. Every person will walk his or her own path, and every person will have to live with his or her own choices.

The truth of the matter is that neither I nor anyone else has a complete and total solution for SSA. But the good news is, based on what I have seen and experienced, we really don't need one in order to carry out our lives and to fulfill our mission as God's *khalifa* on this earth. All we need to have are the key facts. And the key facts are that Allah has created us to worship Him, that He tests each of us with something unique to him or her, that He has concern for us and wants to see us succeed in our path to Him, that He has made certain actions *halal* and others *haram*, that He has given us the gift of moral agency and has made us responsible for our actions, and that, as He has promised us in the Qur'an in numerous verses, He "never burdens a soul with more than it can bear."

We can and we should use whatever means are available out there that work for each of us to control our actions and behavior, as this is what Allah has made us responsible for in front of Him, and to address and work through our various issues as best we can. How our individual lives end up after that, what Allah ultimately has in store for each of us here below (not to mention "there above") when we struggle patiently in His Way, with faith and trust in Him – all of this is in the hands of Allah, our Master, Who says in the Qur'an: "No soul knows what joy is kept hidden for it as a reward for that which they used to do" (Surat al-Sajda, v. 17).

Walking the Straight Path

I think, in sum, that this is a way forward: self-control and self-discipline. And no, I am not saying that we "pray away the gay," but that we learn how to tame and control our *nafs* such that it doesn't govern our actions. This is what Allah has asked of us – no more, but also no less. What happens beyond that is open and is different for each person according to what Allah has decreed. Some may one day find marriage a viable option and go down that path. Others will remain celibate and continue on that path. Some will use their time and their talents to pursue Islamic knowledge and community work and go down that path. Each person's road to Allah is unique and specific to him or her, but we believe firmly in the words of our Lord when He says: "Those who struggle (*jaahadu*) for Our sake, We shall surely guide them to

Our ways. Truly God is with those who practice virtue (*al-muhsineen*)" (Surat al-'Ankabut, v. 69).

As we all affirm as Muslims, Allah's path – which we ask Him to guide us to a minimum of 17 times a day in our daily prayers – is none other than the Straight Path (*al-sirat al-mustaqim*). It is for this reason that we Muslims who have been given the test of same-sex attractions refer to our struggle as the Straight Struggle. In reality, we as Muslims are all engaged in the Straight Struggle – the struggle to remain on the Straight Path of our Lord and Maker. We each have our own challenges to deal with and our own hurdles to overcome along the way, but our road in the end is one, just as our Goal is One.

In reality, we as Muslims are all engaged in the Straight Struggle – the struggle to remain on the Straight Path of our Lord and Maker. We each have our own challenges to deal with and our own hurdles to overcome along the way, but our road in the end is one, just as our Goal is One.

To the Muslim community as a whole I would like to say: the time to act on this issue was yesterday. Let us catch up now, because I might be the person standing next to you in the masjid. I might be your coworker, your friend, your blood brother, or your spouse. I might be your child or your parent. Who knows? I might even be you.

Brother Yousef is a Muslim with same-sex attractions who, along with many other Muslims in his shoes, has committed to living his life on the basis of established Islamic moral and spiritual teachings.

In addition, Br. Yousef has moderated an online support group for same-sex attracted Muslims (www.straightstruggle.com) for the past 13 years, giving him a wealth of experience and a unique perspective from which to address this topic. His essay is addressed to imams, chaplains, Muslim activists and community leaders, to the Muslim community at large, and to other fellow Muslims who find themselves dealing with same-sex desires and attractions.

INFIDELITY AND MISPLACED BLAME IN THE MUSLIM COMMUNITY

By Imam Omar Suleiman

Infidelity is a major topic that too often, like many other embarrassing elements of our community, gets brushed under the rug. Imams routinely have to deal with couples where one spouse is being unfaithful. I don't believe that it's a greater epidemic in the Muslim community than society at large, but it is probably almost just as bad.

It is estimated that roughly 30% to 60% of all married individuals (in the United States) will engage in infidelity at some point during their marriage (Buss & Shackelford 1997). Just like with any community, there are <u>unique complications and considerations</u> when dealing with an issue of this nature. In our community, we have the following:

Belittle & Blame

As a defense mechanism, the cheating spouse will often talk his/her spouse down and belittle them in order to deflect from their own major sin while also gaining sympathy from the onlookers.

Under the influence of cultures that place unfair expectations and blame on the wife, many women are likely to be blamed for not keeping their husbands happy, even at times by their own families. This approach, of course, is completely devoid of any Islamic precedent or Prophetic tradition. The Prophet ﷺ never chastised the spouse of an adulterer for not doing enough to stop them from cheating.

According to John and Julie Gottman's 40 years of marital research, there is one common denominator that tends to begin the cascade toward betrayal in a marriage: When one spouse attempts to connect with the other and the other spouse turns away from this while negatively comparing, this is the first step toward betrayal. A negative comparison sounds something like this, "Who needs this frustration? I could do so much better with someone else." This type of belittling and justification, while imagining oneself as innocent, deteriorates trust and starts people on the downward spiral toward infidelity.

"Righting" Wrongs, Wrongly

Often, men who are unfaithful will try to "right the wrong" by marrying the person they were unfaithful with, at times without even fulfilling the requirements of a marriage. This is where the all too common "secret" second wife comes into the picture.

Or many men ditch the first wife and make it seem like the woman they were cheating with just came into the picture. Alas, even the most practicing Muslims will forsake all principles and beliefs regarding Islamic marriage— holding weird Skype Nikahs — without the most basic conditions of a marriage contract being met. They will then continue to beat up on the first spouse for "making them do it."

The very idea of a *secret* marriage defeats the purpose of marriage. The Prophet ﷺ taught us to publicize marriage for so many different reasons, one of them is that the man with a secret second wife often may have seven or eight other "second wives." In a very awkward scenario that I witnessed a few years ago, a brother in the community sought the help of an Imam to pursue a sister who was secretly married to that very same Imam.

In looking at the research, how many affairs become lasting relationships? Dr. Frank Pittman, an expert on treating affairs, found that the divorce rate of those who marry the person they were unfaithful with is 75%. What was the major reason for these divorces? A lack of trust. How can you trust someone who chose to be with you by cheating on someone they had previously committed to?

Can't Cheat Allah

A piece of advice to the brothers and sisters who are cheating on their spouses: There is no justification for adultery, and victim shaming here won't save you from being held accountable by Allah on the Day of Judgment. No human being will bear the burden of another on the Day of Judgment. Seeking validation from backward cultural elements or friends that are just as unfaithful as you won't change the creed.

Allah says in the Quran in Surah Al-'Isrā' 17:32,

> **"And do not approach unlawful sexual intercourse. Indeed, it is ever an immorality and is evil as a way."**

In an authentic Hadith, the Prophet of Allah ﷺ said: "The one who cheats is not one of us." *Sahih Muslim*

Nothing that started with the deception of Shaytan will suddenly gain the blessing of Allah. If you were unfaithful, you need to sincerely seek forgiveness from your Creator and the people you've hurt with your infidelity. You need to fully accept blame for your sin, and start taking the necessary steps to try to fix things.

Heard It Through the Grapevine- Churning the Rumor Mill

A piece of advice to people who immerse themselves in rumors, there is nothing more sacred than a chaste person's dignity or honor. Yes, there are many that are guilty of the crimes above, but to wrongly accuse one person is enough of a sin in the hereafter to doom you. I'm all for transparency and calling out these social ills, but I reject falsely projecting them on people without proper evidence.

Too Close for Comfort

A piece of advice to those who are starting to get too close and comfy with another person at work or school. The adultery of the private parts is the most severe manifestation of it, but you may already be committing adultery with your tongues, eyes, and hands. Even if you're not physically cheating yet, you may already be emotionally cheating on your spouse. Don't walk the footsteps of shaytan to a place of no return. Cut it off before it goes any further.

According to Dr. Shirley Glass, the dynamics of emotional infidelity result in sexual relationships in 80% of cases. Substituting emotional intimacy, friendship and empathy with someone other than your spouse is not a "platonic" relationship; it is seeking one of the most essential aspects of a marriage outside of it.

Graced By A Cold Shoulder

And most importantly, a piece of advice to those who have been cheated on by their spouses and unjustly blamed for not doing a good enough job to stop your spouse from cheating. It is not your fault that he/she couldn't save themselves from their lowly desires. Allah will not punish you in the hereafter, even if society unjustly does in this world. Even if you have made mistakes, no mistake justifies your spouse making *that* mistake. Don't internalize society's backwardness or your spouse's devilish taunts.

Rise above it all.

Imam Omar Suleiman is the Founder and President of the Yaqeen Institute for Islamic Research, and an Adjunct Professor of Islamic Studies in the Graduate Liberal Studies Program at SMU (Southern Methodist University).

He is also the Resident Scholar at Valley Ranch Islamic Center and Co-Chair of Faith Forward Dallas at Thanks-Giving Square. He holds a Bachelors in Accounting, a Bachelors in Islamic Law, a Masters in Islamic Finance, a Masters in Political History, and is currently pursuing a Phd. in Islamic Thought and Civilization from the International Islamic University of Malaysia.

ON SECRET MARRIAGES

By Sh. Dr. Mohammad Akram Nadwi

Some brothers and sisters have asked me to comment on a practice that is increasingly reported of travelling Muslim scholars and teachers of Islam in the West, and those who travel to the West as teachers and preachers. This is the practice of contracting secret marriages in the places these scholars visit or pass through.

The first thing to be said is that people generally do not make a secret of actions and relations except when they have some sense that these actions and relations, if known, would be disapproved of.

Those who take the responsibility of public teaching of Islam must know that they are seen as representatives of the religion and looked up to as role models. Not only the words they preach, but also their actions and lifestyle influence the decisions and actions of others.

Before God they are liable for that influence and for its consequences in the lives of others. Preachers, teachers, and other public figures in the community, have a responsibility to ensure that their conduct adheres to the ideal of those who fear even to displease God, let alone wilfully disobey His commands or those of His Messenger, upon him be peace.

Every Muslim knows that good deeds repel evil ones, but how many of us are mindful that the converse is also true: that evil deeds can negate, undo or outweigh good ones?

Secret marriage is one of several kinds of violation by men of the rights and dignity of women. I have been informed that it is increasingly common for Muslim preachers in Europe and America and for those visiting the West to marry women in secret and for a short period, after which they, presumably, end the marriage, before going on to contract another marriage of the same sort somewhere else.

This is a violation of the laws and good purposes of marriage, and a vicious exploitation of women whose circumstances oblige them to enter into such contracts. The wrong is analogous to riba, which is a violation of the laws and good purposes of lending money, and severely injurious to those whose circumstances force them to borrow in this illegal way.

Marriage in Islam

Marriage in Islam is presented as a good deed, a noble thing to do, when it is done in the manner and for the purposes described as ma'ruf – i.e., according to the known, established norms of kindness and public, legal form. It is explicit in Surat al-Nisa' that even when a

Muslim contracts a marriage with a slave, he must inform her family and get their consent, and he must pay her the mahr.

What is explicitly forbidden is taking lovers in secret, debauchery, and fornication, i.e., sexual relations without responsibility for the other person and for the consequences of the act. Secret, temporary marriages are a legal cover for what is illegal and known to be so.

Marriage is *both* a personal and social fact for the contracting parties. It is not merely one and not the other. It is an integral part of what makes marriage a good deed that it should be done with the intention of building a legal, social, physical space in which children are to be welcomed and raised.

It is an integral part of what makes marriage a good deed that it connects families not hitherto connected, or it extends and consolidates existing connections. In this way, marriage widens the network of family relations, so that there is multiplicity of siblings and cousins, uncles and aunts and nephews and nieces, among whom responsibility for each other's well-being (physical, economic and spiritual) is shared, usually unevenly, as means and talents and situations are diverse. The social relationships facilitate and diversify, and thereby strengthen and support, the burdens of personal relationship of the husband and wife.

It goes without saying that when a man contracts a marriage he commits himself, in principle, to provide for his wife for her lifetime – it is not lawful for a Sunni

Muslim to contract a marriage knowing in advance that this commitment is temporary.

What distinguishes a marriage as such, what ennobles it above any form of improper association of man and woman, is that it is proclaimed to be a responsible union: marriage proclaims the couple's right to privacy and intimacy with each other, and the purposes of that right.

The neighborhood and community must know the legal status of the couple's being together, so that they can celebrate their relation and support it. Secret marriages, in addition to violating the rights of women, also violate the right of the community to be spared the innuendoes and slanders that are so corruptive of social order, harmony and trust.

The Prophet, peace be upon him, said: 'Proclaim the marriage' (Sunan al-Nasa'i, 3369; Musnad Ahmad, 15697; Sunan Sa`id ibn Mansur, 635).

This a clear injunction that marriages must be proclaimed, made public, not held in secret. That is the practice of the Prophet himself, of all his Companions, and of the prominent scholars of the early generations. None of them ever indulged in secret marriages and they never, explicitly or tacitly, approved any such marriages. Moreso, many of them disapproved of them outright.

We read in al-Mughni, k. al-Nikah that among those who expressed explicit disapproval of secret marriages are: `Umar ibn al-Khattab, `Urwah ibn al-Zubayr, `Ubaydullah ibn `Abdillah ibn `Utbah, `Amir al-Sha`bi. Abu Bakr `Abd al-`Aziz says: 'Such a marriage is void'.

There too we find that the majority of the jurists say that the proclamation of marriage is recommended, i.e., they do not make it a legal condition for the validity of a marriage, assuming that it has been legally witnessed. Some say that proclamation is mandatory.

Even those scholars who do not make proclamation a legal condition for the validity of a marriage do not express approval for keeping it secret. Ibn Taymiyyah, as forceful and forthright as ever, likens secret marriages to prostitution (Majmu` al-fatawa, 32/102).

This is the opinion of al-Zuhri: 'If someone marries secretly, brings two witnesses but commands them to keep it secret, it would be obligatory to separate the husband and wife'. Similarly, it is reported that Imam Malik's opinion is that non-proclamation of marriage invalidates the marriage (al-Mughni, k. al-nikah).

In sum:

Sunni fiqh condemns secret and temporary marriages (secret or public) because they are so injurious to the rights and dignity of women, and because they diminish the good that comes from marriage, namely family life and family relations with all that they provide of testing and training for mind, heart and temperament, and for all the consolations of sharing feelings and experiences across generations.

Contracting secret/temporary marriages reduces marriage to sexual relations in an ugly sort of rental arrangement, that is profoundly demeaning, especially to women. Accordingly, I strongly advise women to be careful before they consent to marry anyone. I strongly advise them to inform, consult with and find support from, family, friends and community before they make any commitments so that the matter is known, and so that their rights are observed and respected. It is better (for women and men) to endure the hardships of being single than to enter into contracts that insult the laws and norms, and seek to subvert the purposes, of marriage as commanded by God and His Messenger, upon him be peace.

As for those who present themselves in public as teachers and preachers of Islam and yet have entered into such contracts, what can I say? It is obligatory for them that they refresh their intentions in due fear of God and that they remember that the door to repentance, to reform, and to making amends, is not closed.

God's Messenger has affirmed in many places that God loves to forgive His creatures if they turn to Him. He makes the way to forgiveness easy for whoever repents sincerely. No believer's sins, however great or numerous, can be greater than His mercy.

Shaykh Mohammad Akram Nadwi is an Islamic scholar from the Indian city of Jaunpur and a graduate of the world renowned Nadwatul Ulama (India) where he studied and taught Shariah.

Shaykh Akram is a Muhaddith has specialized in Ilm ul Rijal (the study of the narrators of Hadith). Shaykh Akram Nadwi has a doctorate in Arabic Language and has authored and translated over 25 titles on Language, Jurisprudence, Qur'an and Hadith.

In May 2010, he completed a monumental 457-volume work on the lives of female scholars of Hadith in Islamic History. Shaykh Akram is the recipient of the Allama Iqbal prize for contribution to Islamic thought. Shaykh Akram is a former research fellow at the Oxford Centre for Islamic Studies, Oxford. He is the Dean and the Academic Director of the Cambridge Islamic College.

WHEN HE LEAVES FOR HER: AN UNACCEPTED REALITY IN OUR COMMUNITIES

By Umm Aasiya

I'll never forget the morning I found out that my husband was having an emotional affair with one of my close friends. They were sharing intimate thoughts, desires, and feelings of love with each other. I paced back and forth in the living room where the memories we made were now broken.

My first reaction was to ask him. He wasn't going to lie. After all, this was the man I trusted more than anything, and he would be the one that would have answers. Little did I know that he was also the man that was going to cause me extraordinary amounts of pain through the choices he made.

See, Muslims assume that emotional or physical affairs never happen in the Muslim community. I assumed they didn't either. But they do, and more often than we'd like to admit.

Things had been fairly normal between my husband and I. We had the usual arguments from time to time, but what marriage doesn't have that? Nothing major had seemed wrong at all, so when I found out about my husband's relationship with another woman, I blamed myself for it all. All the flaws I thought I had were suddenly magnified in my own eyes.

Why I Stayed

I am not a believer in the statement: "Once a cheater, always a cheater." I wholeheartedly believe people have the ability to change when they're given a chance, and sometimes that's all some people need. A chance.

So I made the conscious decision to stay with my husband and give him another chance. I told myself that I wanted to work things through, that I wanted to stay and fight to save my marriage. I was determined to make it better than it ever was before. So I gave him one chance.

And another.

And another.

With each failed chance I found more details revealing the emotional involvement that was still ongoing. With each new detail, a wound that had barely started healing was torn open again. Each tear took longer to heal, and before I knew it I was on the road to self-destruction.

There were countless times my husband was dishonest about what was going on, but I believed him. My blind faith and belief in him came from the amount of trust I put in this man. I had married him based on faith and character, not for money or career. He played a big role within his community, and many spoke very highly of him.

He was such a good man, he had such high standards-and it was because of those high standards that I could not accept that he would consciously cause me so much pain. Therefore I blamed myself.

So did he.

I was made to feel crazy for having suspicions, even when my suspicions turned out to be correct. I was told I was the one that needed serious help, and that I needed to get my issues under control.

In my desperation to make things work I made myself extremely vulnerable. Some may even say I was being naïve. But there I was, ready and willing give all I had in me to save my marriage and the man I had committed myself to. At the end of the day, his heart was somewhere else, but I have no regrets. I know I did everything I possibly could in order to make my marriage work.

It Really Was For Her

Soon after our divorce, he married her.

Finding out made me feel validated - I wasn't a crazy woman for suspecting his emotional affair was ongoing. I wasn't wrong for doubting him when he said he didn't want her.

Being right was satisfying, but it also tore me apart. Seeing him get married to the woman who broke my home, my family, my life. This woman who had been my friend, my confidant. A sister of mine through Islam. It turned out this woman was really my enemy.

This woman told my husband how much she loved him. This woman wore my husband's pajamas to bed at night. This woman was now living in the same space that I had shared with my husband.

The man I trusted, respected, and married believing I would spend my entire life with - he married this woman. And now, he was her husband instead.

I don't know what was worse, living through the affair or being destroyed by the losing fight to save my marriage. I live in the pain of silence while they continue with their lives as though nothing wrong was done. People within my own community accept them and what they've done. His family, that I was once a part of, is silent about my disappearance and replacement.

Maybe. Just Maybe

Maybe I should've spoken up instead of trying to protect him. Maybe I should've confronted her when I had the chance. Maybe I should've done something differently, maybe if I was just stronger…maybe maybe maybe.

I can make a long list out of things I should've or could've done differently. Or, I can accept that this was all part of Allah's plan. Like all struggles we go through, we have to remember there is a bigger plan behind the things that happen to us.

Maybe we think we have the perfect plan for our lives... get married, have kids, have an amazing career, and when those things don't work out for us, we fall into deep depression and disappointment. What we fail to see is that Allah took those things away from us because He is planning to replace what we lost with something better.

"Do they think that they will be left to say "We believe," and they will not be tried?" [Ankabut:29].

We have to leave it to the One who has the power to create all good, and trust that He will give us good in ways that we never imagined.

To the Woman Dealing with Her Husband's Affair

"No person earns any sin except against himself, and no bearer of burdens shall bear the burden of another." Surah Al-Anam 164

If you're currently in this situation, please put the burden of blame down before it sets in permanently. We're all grownups here, and he should never blame someone else for his actions. Flaws in a marriage call for mercy, communication, and compromise - not infidelity.

> *As a defense mechanism, the cheating spouse will often talk his/her spouse down and belittle them in order to deflect from their own major sin while also gaining sympathy from the onlookers" –Sheikh Omar Suleiman*

Take care of yourself. Do not neglect your emotional, mental, or physical well-being. Build yourself back up and remember that Allah does not burden any one more than they can bear.

"Allah does not place a burden on a soul greater than it can bear." —Surah Baqarah, 286

It will feel unbearable at times. You may feel like ending it all, or feel like you have nothing left to live for, but in those vulnerable moments, remember that no one understands your pain more than Allah.

When others run out of words of comfort, or begin to understand your pain, remember that Allah understands your heartbreak.

Be Bigger

Allah says: "And who is better in speech than the one who invites to Allah and does righteousness and says, 'Indeed, I am of the Muslims.' And not are equal the good deed and the bad. Repel evil by that which is better." [Fussilat: 33-34]

No matter how much it hurts, keep this in mind: We are commanded to repel evil by doing that which is BEST. It will be hard, but it is crucial that you remember that the reward given to those that have patience in times of hardship is a reward given without measure.

There is a fine line between being patient and staying no matter how bad his treatment of you gets, and how little he cares about rebuilding your trust. If you see no hope for a change to the positive, you should stand up for yourself and know that Allah has something better in store for you.

Dr. Neil Warren, author of Triumphant Marriage, says: "...75 percent of all divorces involve marriages in which at least one partner is emotionally unhealthy." No matter how much you would like to or how much you try, if the unhealthy individual is not willing to own the problem, confess it, or seek personal restorations, the marriage is headed for disaster.

To the Woman Involved with a Married Man

No matter how much you try to convince yourself that what you're doing is justifiable, it is not. If a man is married, regardless of what excuses he gives you, it is not okay to get emotionally or physically involved.

Put yourself into the situation of the woman whose husband you're "having a good time with." Could you trust a man who snuck behind his wife's back? Knowing that he treats his wife in such a way, how could you trust him if you were his wife instead?

Know that this man left his first wife by lying and cheating on her. Know that you are not safe from such behavior.

If you do go through with it all and marry this man, know that you are responsible for destroying the life of another woman and breaking up a family. Congratulations, you're doing shaytaan's work for him.

The Prophet ﷺ said: "Iblis places his throne upon water; he then sends detachments (for creating dissension between people); the nearer to him in rank are those who are most notorious in creating dissension. One of them comes and says: "I did so and so." And he says: "You have done nothing." Then one amongst them comes and says: "I did not spare so and so until I sowed the seed of discord between a husband and a wife." Shaytaan goes near him and says: "You have done well." He then embraces him" (Sahih Muslim; narrated by Jabir Ibn 'Abdullah).

Even if you care nothing for the betrayed wife, remember that you're trying to marry someone who cheated on their spouse. Someone who didn't like what they had at home so they went looking for something better. When your honeymoon wears off, will he go looking for that better someone?

It doesn't really matter who started it. It doesn't matter if you were tricked and didn't know at first that he had a wife at home waiting for him. At the end of the day, Allah knows all the details, He is constantly watching, and everything will be laid out in front of you on the Day of Judgment. Stop it while you still have control, and gain some dignity.

If you don't do it for anyone else, do it for Allah's sake. Remember, "...He is with you wherever you are, and He is seeing of what you do." (57:4)

End the affair to please Him, and He will give you something better.

The Only Way is Up

In the end I've learned that once you hit rock bottom, the only way is up. I can say now that life after such a sordid affair does get better, but, it only gets better with time. In the moment everything is happening you will feel broken and shattered, but everything you go through has a purpose, and it will make you stronger than ever before if you let it.

When we hit our rock bottom, we have to remember that if we turn to Allah, He will make a way out for us, no matter how lost we may feel. My personal journey and struggle is still ongoing but I see glimmers of bright and sunny days ahead, InshaAllah. I will continue to persevere.

I see now the chance that Allah has given me to make myself into a better person, one who has Allah as a Protector, Guide, and Confidant. I am learning to leave it all to Allah, because at the end of the day He knows what's best for us and we know nothing. In Him I put my trust, and let all those that trust, put their trust in Him. (12:67)

Umm Aasiya is the pen-name of a sister who shared her story with MuslimMatters.org on the condition of anonymity.